Going Bananas!
A Kid's Guide To Puerto Limon, Costa Rica

Photography by John D. Weigand
Poetry by Penelope Dyan

Bellissima Publishing, LLC
Jamul, California
www.bellissimapublishing.com

Copyright © 2019 by Penny D. Weigand & John D. Weigand

All rights reserved. No part of this book may be
reproduced or transmitted in any form or by any means,
electronic or mechanical, including photocopying,
recording, or by any other means, or by any information or
storage retrieval system, without permission from the publisher.

ISBN 978-1-61477-381-8
First Edition

"It's always fun to go bananas!"

PENELOPE DYAN

Going Bananas!
Bellissima Publishing, LLC

Introduction

Puerto Limon, one of the most picturesque places in Costa Rica, sits right between Nicaragua and Panama, with lots of coconut trees, and (of course) bananas! And if you are lucky, you might see a monkey; and you might even see even a sloth hanging from or in a tree! Famous for bananas, if you happen to go on a guided tour of the region, you will hear all about the history of bananas in this region; and you may even get to taste a banana ripened by Limon's tropical sun! So, if you are going to go bananas, or if you decide to even go for bananas, (or perhaps anther tropical fruit) this is the perfect place for you to be! The people are friendly, and the dress is almost always casual! After all, you are only a hop, skip and a jump away from the beach, so even if Mom and Dad dress up to go out at night, chances are you won't have to put on anything to wear except for your swimsuit, or shorts and a t-shirt, or a sundress (if you are a girl, of course).

This is a fun, 'learn to read' book filled with word repetition, word recognition and rhyme, written by award winning author, attorney and former teacher, Penelope Dyan; and it is meant to give you a kid's eye glimpse of Puerto Limon. There is also a free music video that goes with this book you can find on Bellissimavideo's YouTube channel.

Going Bananas!
Bellissima Publishing, LLC

Going Bananas!
A Kid's Guide To Puerto Limon, Costa Rica

Photography by John D. Weigand
Poetry by Penelope Dyan

Mom says that there are a lot of things in Puerto Limon to see, and if you are VERY lucky, you might EVEN see a MONKEY hiding high up in a tree!

Bananas hang from trees here,
sometimes ripening in blue plastic bags;
AND what's more,
you can ALSO buy bananas
(just like THESE bananas)
from a fruit stand,
OR from a local store!

There's A LOT of fruit here
that YOU can buy AND eat,
fruit that is delicious AND ripe,
fruit that is oh so very SWEET!

Mom tells you to look up high
into a tree that NEARLY touches
the blue of the Caribbean sky!
And then lo and behold!
What is it that you SEE?
YOU see a Caribbean monkey
hiding HIGH up in that TREE!

In a store,
your mom buys a toy sloth for YOU!
AND she ALSO buys a toy sloth
for your SISTER,
because of toy sloths
(in this store)
there just happen to be TWO!

You find a golden mermaid
not so VERY far from the sea.
You wonder about the pirates of old,
and about the things of the future
that just MIGHT be!

You walk right down to the beach.
You see, it is VERY close!
AND it is NOT too hard to REACH!
And as you gaze out at the water,
you wonder how AND why . . .
the blue of Puerto Limon's
Caribbean water
seems to touch
the blue of Puerto Limon's
Caribbean sky!

Your mom buys your SISTER
a toy parrot.
And THEN Dad buys YOU a ball!
They have to reach up
to get them down from the shelf,
because you and Sis
just aren't very TALL!

You pass right by a nearby lagoon, and mom sadly tells you, "We'll be leaving here soon!"

Then you make one MORE stop,
and DAD complains,
because MOM wants (again) to shop!
Your sister gets excited.
Dad asks,
"Why ALL the fuss?"
And Mom buys you AND your sister
(each) a brightly colored toy bus!

Mom tries to convince you
this is a ONLY a chocolate treat,
but this is something that looks ICKY,
AND so (of this) YOU refuse to eat!
The man at the counter tells you
there are cocoa beans inside,
as behind your mother's skirt
you desperately TRY to HIDE!
Your sister decides it is ONLY right,
that she NOT try it
unless YOU first take a bite!

As the sun sets upon the sea,
a brand new adventure lies ahead.
AND you think about THIS,
as your mother tucks you into bed.
You think about the setting sun
and its reflection on the sea.
AND you think about that monkey
you saw so high up in that TREE!
And when you finally
close your eyes to sleep,
you think about
that beautiful golden mermaid . . .
and about
the silent creatures of the deep.

"Every day of your life is a new adventure!
And this is how it should be!"

PENELOPE DYAN

www.ingramcontent.com/pod-product-compliance
Ingram Content Group UK Ltd.
Pitfield, Milton Keynes, MK11 3LW, UK
UKHW060133240426

12048UKWH00002B/16

Here & There
A Kid's Guide to Southwick UK

Photography By John D. Weigand
Poetry By Penelope Dyan

Bellissima Publishing, LLC
Jamul, California
www.bellissimapublishing.com

Copyright © 2020 by Penny D. Weigand and John D. Weigand

All rights reserved. No part of this book may be
reproduced or transmitted in any form or by any means,
electronic or mechanical, including photocopying,
recording, or by any other means, or by any information or
storage retrieval system, without permission from the publisher.

ISBN 978-1-61477-444-0
First Edition

"There is something new to see and learn everywhere you happen to go"

PENELOPE DYAN

Here & There
Bellissima Publishing, LLC

Introduction

During the Second World War almost all of the Allied forces operational planning was done in London. However, The plans for D-Day were finalized at Southwick House in Hampshire, led by General Dwight D. Eisenhower, who later became the 34th President of the United States of America. And the fact is that the entire Southwick village was taken over by Allied command. So let this little book carry you up the road into to the village of Southwick and right back down!

This 'learn to read' book' takes a look at history, as you are guided through its pages by photographer John D. Weigand and the award winning author, attorney and former teacher, Penelope Dyan. Have fun exploring Southwick (pronounced as "Suth-ick") as you build your reading word vocabulary and reading skills through word recognition, word repetition and rhyme. See some of what General Eisenhower saw, as you go on an exploration of the past; and just let your imagination run wild!

To see more of Southwick, go to Bellissimavideo's YouTube channel and watch the free music video that goes with this book!

Here & There
Bellissima Publishing, LLC

Here & There
A Kid's Guide to Southwick UK

Photography By John D. Weigand
Poetry By Penelope Dyan

There is a sign that points the way.
Dad says,
"It looks like this will be
a very, very, very fun day!"
Mom makes a face and says,
"I think I just might get bus ride sick,
if we don't get to where we are going;
and if we don't get there quick!"

There is another sign on the road.
I wonder what LORRIES are.
"They are trucks," I am told.
Then our guide says cars in the UK
travel on the left side of the road!
He says the left side is right,
and the right side is wrong.
Mom says,
"You'll probably be thinking about THAT
all day long!"

Dad laughs and soon
we come to another sign.
And that sign says, "GIVE WAY".
Mom laughs and says,
"It's turning out to be a very, very, very
interesting day!"

We come across a house
with a thatched roof;
and we are told,
"These thatched roofs will last until
they are FIFTY years old!"

And then . . . as we rumble along
in our tour bus,
the kid in the seat behind me
starts to make a very, very big FUSS!
Dad says to Mom,
"Did you know, my dear,
that General Dwight D. Eisenhower
led the Allied forces
on D-Day right from HERE?"

There is a great big, giant cannon!
What a sight to see!
But I would NOT like that great big,
giant cannon pointed
at mom OR at dad OR at ME!
I decided right then and there
that war was very, very, very BAD!
And THEN, when I thought of people
dying in ANY war,
it made me very, very, very SAD!
And THEN dad told me
during World War II it was only right,
because it was pure evil
that good men HAD to fight.

I asked if General Eisenhower
and his men ever shopped here.
Mom said,
"I think it is very, very, very likely
that General Eisenhower and his men
did shop here, my dear."
I smiled and I imagined that great man
walking down this VERY street;
and then I looked up at dad and I said,
"This place is so NEAT!"
And by that I meant
(when all was said and all was done)
that coming HERE was very, very, very
interesting and FUN!

And then we went
to the D-Day museum;
and right there on a hill
stood a lighthouse and a fortress,
both quite silent and quite still.

And as we traveled on down the road,
'We're going to a place called Seaside,"
I was quite simply told.

And then as we drew closer to the sea,
I imagined how very, very, frightening
World War II had to be . . .
especially when it came to kids,
kids that were just like ME!
And so I asked my dad something
that I had NEVER asked anyone before.
I asked my dad quite simply
and very, very, very quietly,
"Why do grown-ups have to make war?"

And as we came to Spice Island,
where merchants of old traded in spice,
I asked my dad,
"Do people make war,
because they are just NOT very nice?"
And my dad quite simply said,
as he scratched his nearly bald head,
"If everyone really loved one another,
AND if everyone really DID care,
maybe kindness and goodness
would teach everyone to SHARE!
AND if everyone could simply
do away with greed,
THEN perhaps going to war would be
an old-fashioned, obsolete need!"

Then dad explained,
"By obsolete, I mean old and useless and out of date."
I shook my head, and hoped that for lasting peace it was NOT too late!
AND I thought of those thatched roofs and those gingerbread looking houses
that were built and were long-standing upon that Southwick hill;
and I said, "I hope someday lasting peace will really, truly come."
And then mom added,
"I pray for YOU that it WILL!"

"Necessity is the mother of invention. Perhaps necessity will someday also be the mother of lasting peace"

PENELOPE DYAN

www.ingramcontent.com/pod-product-compliance
Ingram Content Group UK Ltd.
Pitfield, Milton Keynes, MK11 3LW, UK
UKHW060133240426
12048UKWH00002B/17